HELL

How could a loving God send anyone there?

bethjones MINISTRIES

HELL - How could a loving God send anyone there?
ISBN: 978-1-933433-09-7

■

Copyright © 2007 Beth Ann Jones

Published by Beth Jones Ministries
2500 Vincent Dr., Portage, MI 49024
800-596-0379   bethjones.org

Printed in the United States of America.
ALL RIGHTS RESERVED.

■

HELL

How could a loving God
send anyone there?

beth jones
MINISTRIES

bethjones
MINISTRIES

bethjones.org

Contents

■ Find The Chapter

Chapter One

■ In Denial About Hell?

Who wants to hear about hell? Not too many people I know. Most of us would prefer to put our fingers in our ears and go, *"Lalalalalalala,"* so we don't have to hear about this awful place. When I say, "Hell," you say, "No"—hell no! Yup, that's what most people think of the subject.

Hell No!

Hell. It's a subject no one wants to talk about, primarily, because we don't want to believe such a place exists. We can't imagine a loving God allowing anyone to go there. It's easier to go into denial about hell.

Are you in denial about hell?

In some ways, I really wish I didn't believe in hell. I really wish I wasn't writing a book about the subject. Living in denial about hell would be easier. I wouldn't have to think about myself or people I love—and where we'll spend eternity. I wouldn't feel any responsibility for telling anyone the news they really don't want to hear.

■ I Don't Want To Hear About It

No one wants to hear about hell—at least, not while they feel immortal, indestructible, and invincible. Most people prefer denial—for a while—until they breathe their last breath and reality kicks in. But, then it's too late.

So, while we're still breathing, why don't we explore the subject we'd prefer to ignore?

Let's talk about it.

What really happens after this life? What happens after we breathe our last breath? When we are six feet under, where are we? Do we just cease to exist? Are we reincarnated? Do we all go to heaven? Does anyone really go to hell?

Is there a hell?

If you've seen news anchors, talk show hosts, tabloid headlines, or watched specials on heaven, there are plenty of debates on heaven and hell. Recently, I saw a talk show promo where the topic was: Heaven and Hell. *"Heaven is a place where I am happy, content, and at peace,"* said one TV personality. *"Hell is earth's worst—famine, war, and terror,"* said another person. The promo ended with this comment:

"In the end, it doesn't matter what we think. God wins!" Is that true?

These are the age-old questions people enjoy theorizing about; but let's bring it a little closer to home: YOU.

What do YOU believe about heaven?
What do YOU believe about hell?

■ Where Will You Go Forever?

Where will YOU be forever? Where will YOU go after this life? Will YOU cease to exist? Will YOU go to heaven? Or, will YOU go to hell?

Perhaps, you don't know. It may be a topic you've never thought about. It's possible you don't care, but I doubt it. Everyone cares; although everyone won't admit it. Is your eternal destination a mystery?

Some people are a bit cavalier in their attitude about hell. Their smug response is, *"Fine, I'll just go to hell and party with all of my friends!"* Sadly, hell won't be the party they hoped for.

Others are just plain honest, *"Yup, for all the stuff I've done, I deserve to go hell."* Still, others are arrogant and obnoxious, *"I wouldn't want to know a God that lets anyone go to hell. If that's the kind of God He is then He can take a flying leap!"*

Maybe you're in another group—you're a believer. Jesus is the Lord of your life, His blood has cleansed you from all your sins, and you're confident that you'll go to heaven and miss hell. That's great. How about your loved ones? Do you have family or friends that are uncertain? Does their eternal destiny hang in the balance?

■ What's The Bottom Line?

Perhaps, when you boil it down, the real reason people are in denial about hell is because they cannot comprehend this question: *How could a loving God send anyone to hell? Forever?*

Let me shock you with an answer. The answer to that question is simple: *A loving God doesn't!* Yes, there is a place called, *hell*; but God is not sending people there. It's true; some people will end up in hell, but not because of God's choice.

God doesn't send people to hell! He's trying to prevent anyone from going there! God's the One who sent the rescue mission, through Jesus Christ, so that no one would have to go to hell.

Here's the truth.

If anybody goes to hell, it's because they've chosen to reject God's Savior—Jesus Christ. They did not want to be "saved." God will honor our choice. People can go to hell if they want to; after all, we have a free will and God won't violate that—more on that topic in our next chapter. For now, brace yourself as we have an honest, frank, and Biblical discussion about a place we'd all rather deny—a place called hell.

Chapter Two

█ The Facts Of Death

I opened my e-mail and read this:

> "Hi, I just thought I'd let you know that my husband's mom passed away last night. She was hospitalized about two weeks ago for frequent falls and weakness. It seemed like one body system after another would quit working. We went to visit her on Sunday, which was Mother's Day, and she was pretty alert but very weak. She died very peacefully late last night. You probably remember my

husband told you that he was able to pray with his mom a few months ago and she accepted Christ as her Savior. We are at peace knowing she is in heaven."

I am not sure there is a better way to cope with life—or death—than to know our loved ones have made peace with God and are spending eternity with Him in heaven. Honestly, I don't know how those without Christ deal with the grief death brings. Death is one reality no one can escape. It's true; 100% of us will die and go somewhere for eternity!

Let's talk about the facts of death.

Just the facts.

■ Everyone Is Afraid To Die

In reality, the Bible says that everybody fears death. *"Because God's children are human beings—made of flesh and blood—Jesus also became flesh and blood by being born in human form. For only as a human being could he die, and only by dying could he break the power of the Devil, who had the power of death. Only in this way could he deliver* **those who have lived all their lives as slaves to the fear of dying,"** (Hebrews 2:14-15, NLT).

Ecclesiastes 7:2 makes it plain, *"For death is the destiny of every man; the living should take this to heart,"* (NIV). Whether consciously or unconsciously, everyone has an awareness of eternity and an internal fear of death. If death is certain and if we are going to go somewhere for eternity, we really ought to pay attention to this reality!

Eternity is a LONG time!

If you live to be 70, 80, 90, or 100 years old, it's still a blip on the radar screen of eternity. One day, you are here on planet Earth and the next day . . . poof! You are gone and somewhere for eternity! Eternity . . . Get the idea? Millions and billions of years . . . and more.

Did you know the only thing that allows you to live on earth "legally" is a body? When your body dies, you can't stay on the earth any longer—legally. You have to leave. As soon as your body dies, the real you—the person that lives behind your eyeballs—has to go somewhere forever. You leave planet Earth and you go somewhere . . . heaven or hell. Those are the only two options the Bible gives us.

Can you absolutely know where you will go when you die? Yes, God has given us the map!

■ MapQuest

The Bible gives us the "Mapquest" for heaven. Listen to what we are told. *"And this is what God has testified: He has given us eternal life, and this life is in his Son.* **So whoever has God's Son has life; whoever does not have his Son does not have life. I write this to you who believe in the Son of God, so that you may know you have eternal life,"** (1 John 5:11-13, NLT).

It's pretty clear, right?

God has given us eternal life, and this life is in His Son. Whoever has the Son, has the life. He that doesn't have the Son doesn't have life.

Need more detail? *"Jesus answered, 'I am the way and the truth and the life. **No one comes to the Father except through me,"** (John 14:6, NIV).*

Jesus is the only way to the Father and heaven! If you have the Son—Jesus is the Lord of your life and you are trusting in His blood—you have eternal life. That's the only way.

Our good deeds don't get us to heaven. Our church attendance doesn't do it. Even our loving life and kindness to others won't get us into heaven. The password for heaven is simple: Jesus. That's it! (For more details on this subject, I encourage you to read the book I wrote titled, DEATH: What Happens Next?)[1]

Remember John 3:16? You've seen it on banners at football games, right? *"For God so loved the world that he gave his only Son, **so***

that everyone who believes in him will not perish but have eternal life," (NLT).

> We see where believers go.
> Where do unbelievers go?

The Bible also gives us the road map for hell. *"I saw the dead, both great and small, standing before God's throne. And the books were opened, including the Book of Life. And the dead were judged according to the things written in the books, according to what they had done.* **And anyone whose name was not found recorded in the Book of Life was thrown into the lake of fire,"** (Revelation 20:12 and 15, NLT).

Anyone whose name is not found in the Lamb's Book of Life will spend their eternal destiny in hell also called "the lake of fire."

I hate this.
It's sad, but true.

■ Hell Won't Be A Big Party

I know, there is this huge temptation to say, *"Yeah, right. I just don't believe it. Life on this earth is hell enough? Get real . . . God has books? A lake of fire? What is this, some kind of 'hellfire and brimstone'? Another Christian preaching damnation in hell . . .blah, blah, blah . . . "*

Or perhaps, as I've mentioned, you have the attitude of, *"Fine, I don't give a rip. I'll just go to hell and party with my friends!"* Listen, hell is not going to be the party you're expecting.

Think about this reality. Heaven is recording your life. God has books. He has a big library and there is one very important book—the Lamb's Book of Life. When you truly surrender your heart and invite Jesus Christ to be the Lord of your life, your name is written in the Lamb's Book of Life. That's the only way your name gets written in the Book. Your name is either in it or it's not. Trust me; this is a Book you want your name to be in!

If your name is not in the Book, it's bad news. Those who choose to disobey God and reject Jesus will face a terrifying future.

I realize there are those who say, *"You're just trying to scare people!"* You're right! You are absolutely correct. Hell is a terrible reality and I hope the truth *"scares the hell right out of you"!*

Perhaps, you need a good scare!

■ Scare Tactics

I was working in our yard with my two young sons and we were trimming branches with an electric chainsaw. I had never used one before, but I knew I needed to be careful. I put on gloves and goggles and was being very conscious to keep my fingers away from the chain!

My boys were watching me and after a while they decided they, too, wanted to use the chainsaw. Immediately, I knew I had to put the "fear of chainsaws" into their minds, so they weren't even tempted to use it. The last thing I wanted my boys to do was to have a cavalier attitude regarding the chainsaw. I didn't want them to come home from school one day and start playing with it.

I put the fear of the chainsaw in the minds of my 6 and 8 year-old boys by saying, *"Listen,* don't you ever use this chainsaw! One slip and you could cut your fingers right off and the doctors might not be able to put them back on. Do you hear what I'm saying? Stay away from this chainsaw!" I wanted to scare them! Maybe I went a little overboard, but you get the idea. Because of that, they have steered clear of the chainsaw.

This idea of hell . . . it is sobering. That's for sure. The hope is that, at some point, you seriously ask yourself, "Is this true? Is there really a place called hell?"

Sometimes the truth is a bummer—at first. In the end, the truth is your best friend. Which would you rather be? Politically incorrect or eternally locked up in hell? I hope you make a decision to steer clear of this place of torment.

■ Are You A Statistic?

Here's one reason this whole subject is so incredibly sobering to me. The Barna Research Group (www.barna.org) conducts extensive research on the beliefs, trends, and opinions of people and their faith. Their research shows, "Thirty-six percent (36%) of the adult population classify themselves as born again, but not evangelical."[2] In Barna studies, "born again" Christians are not defined on the basis of characterizing themselves as "born again," but based upon their answers to two questions.

The first question is: *"Have you ever made a personal commitment to Jesus Christ that is still important in your life today?"* If the respondent says, "Yes," then they are asked a follow-up question about life after death. One of the seven responses a respondent may choose is: *"When I die, I will go to heaven because I have confessed my sins and have accepted Jesus Christ as my Savior."*

Individuals who answer, "Yes," to the first question and select this statement as their belief about their own salvation are then categorized as "born again."

According to Barna, 36% of the adults in America, "the Christian nation," are classified as born again believers. That means 65% of the population are non-believers. This boils down to the reality that two-thirds of the population in America have not made a commitment to Jesus Christ that is still important in their lives today. Two-thirds of the people said that when they die, they will not go to heaven because they've not confessed their sins and accepted Jesus Christ as their Savior.

Think about these ramifications.
Do the math.

Experts tell us over 2,400,000 Americans die in America each year.[3] That means, 6,575 Americans die every day. Approximately 40% of these deaths are sudden. Each day, thousands of people wake up fully expecting to live long lives and by the end of the day 6,575 people are gone! When people leave planet Earth, they will go somewhere.

Where do they go?

Of the 2.4 million Americans that will die this year, it's very possible that 65% of those people do not believe in Jesus Christ. Heaven has no record of their reservation. Their names are not written in the Lamb's Book of Life and they will not enter through the pearly gates according to the Bible. That means, it's very likely that this year, 1.5 million people will die and find themselves eternally checked-in to a place called hell.

Does this alarm you?
It should!

I hope it alarms you enough to think about your own eternity and that of your family, friends, and loved ones! What about your co-workers? Neighbors? What about everyone you're connected to?

■ God Is Not Sending People To Hell

I know some of you are not convinced. You're still thinking, *"C'mon, how could a loving God send anyone to hell?"*

Again, the answer to that question is this: A loving God doesn't. God doesn't send people to hell! God's the One that sent the rescue mission, through Jesus Christ, so that no one would have to go. If anyone goes to hell, it's because they chose to reject God's rescue plan through Jesus Christ. God gives us a free will to choose light or darkness, life or death, heaven or hell.

Let's look at John 3:16-20, *"For God so loved the world that he gave his one and only Son, that whoever believes in him shall not perish but have eternal life.* **For God did not send his Son into the world to condemn the world, but to save the world through him.** *Whoever believes in him is not condemned,* **but whoever does not believe stands condemned already because he has not believed in the name of God's one and only Son. This is the verdict: Light has come into the world,**

but men loved darkness instead of light because their deeds were evil. *Everyone who does evil hates the light, and will not come into the light for fear that his deeds will be exposed,"* (NIV).

Jesus is the Savior, not the destroyer!

No wonder Jesus told us to "go" and preach the gospel to this crazy world! We are supposed to be working with God to let people know the Good News: they don't have to go to hell! There is a Savior!

I received this letter from a gal years ago. She had been a Christian for about a year and a half. This is her story in her own words.

"I thought present-day life was hell. I was born out of wedlock, adopted into an unloving family, and literally picked

myself up more often than not because of unsatisfactory behavior. In our family, the Bible was just a book that held the family tree information. All of that changed one day, when a friend of mine was diagnosed with cancer.

He was a proud man, recently retired, financially sound, and looking forward to the future. When he became sick, he put his house on the market and moved closer to the best specialist in hope of help. The truth was, there was no hope. As he became sicker, he became more bitter—and so did his daughter and wife.

Slowly and methodically, his body shut down, but not his mind. He knew no God and professed only his fear of the demons. In his last days, he neither drank nor ate due to his inability; yet, he refused

*to die. Hospice personnel said they had
never seen anyone so afraid to die.*

*Finally, the end did come, but it was not
the calm environment one would hope
for. It was one of sheer terror. He left
earth screaming to his daughter to not
let them take him. She said it was as if
he saw the demons in the wait and his
anxiety was ever-present as he plead for
one more breath."*

This gal saw the reality of someone that didn't
know the Lord going into eternity lost, she
gave it great consideration and ultimately it
moved her to choose Jesus.

*Hell is a real place.
    It's not a party.
        You don't want to go there.*

Who's Who In Hell – Part 1

Who's who in hell? Is the roster just made up of earth's obvious scumbags? The Bible tells us all about hell's guest list.

Do not get on this list.

The Devil And His Demons

Did you know hell was never meant for people? It was prepared for the devil and his angels. It was never God's desire to send man to the place called hell. Initially, the devil was the only rebel in the universe and God created a penitentiary for him and his demons.

Jesus revealed hell's original purpose when He spoke about the final judgement.

"Then he will say to those on his left, 'Depart from me, you who are cursed, into the eternal fire prepared for the devil and his angels,'" (Matthew 25:41, NIV).

Sadly, man has also rebelled against God and His plan of salvation and those who reject Jesus will also spend eternity in hell.

■ Those Without Christ

It's true. Those without Christ will be on hell's roster. Maurice Rawlings, a cardiologist, wrote *Beyond Death's Door*, based on events that happened in his emergency room. When cardiac arrest patients came to the hospital and had death and near-death experiences, he recorded these accounts in his book.[1]

Here's one story that changed his life, and it's what prompted him to write a book. He describes a 40 year-old white, male patient. He was a rural mail carrier of medium build, dark-haired and had a personality that would please anyone.

Here's what Dr. Rawlings wrote:

> *"Unfortunately, he represented one of those rare instances where the EKG not only went haywire, but his heart stopped altogether. He had a cardiac arrest and dropped dead right at my office." Dr. Rawlings described what they began to try to do, when he wrote, "… I started external heart massage by pushing on his chest. One nurse initiated mouth-to-mouth breathing, another nurse found a breathing mask, still another nurse brought*

in pace maker equipment. Unfortunately, the heart would not maintain its own beat. I had to insert a pace maker wire, and the patient began coming to. Each time he regained heartbeat and respiration, the patient screamed, 'I am in hell!' He was terrified and pleaded with me to help him. I was scared to death."

"He then issued a very strange plea. The patient said not to stop on this external heart massage. He said, 'Don't stop!' I noticed a genuinely alarmed look on his face. He had a terrified look, worse than the expression seen in death. This patient had a grotesque grimace, expressing sheer horror. His pupils were dilated and he was perspiring and trembling. He looked as if his hair was on end."

Dr. Rawlings said this patient said, "'Don't you understand? I am in hell! Each time you quit, I go back to hell. Don't let me go back to hell!' Being accustomed to patients under this kind of stress, I dismissed his complaint. I said, 'Don't bother me about your hell until I finish getting this pace maker in place.' But the man was serious and it finally occurred to me that he was indeed in trouble. By this time, the patient had experienced three or four episodes of complete unconsciousness and clinical death from both cessation of heartbeat and breathing."

"After several death episodes, the man said, 'How do I stay out of hell?' I told him I guessed it was the same principle I learned in Sunday school. I guessed Jesus Christ would be one to whom you would have to ask to save you. This patient said, 'I don't know how. Pray for me.' Pray for him?

What nerve! I told him I was a doctor and not a preacher. 'Pray for me,' he repeated. I knew I had no choice. It was a dying man's request. So, I had him repeat these words after me. It was very simple. I told him it went something like this. 'Lord Jesus, I ask you to keep me out of hell. Forgive my sins. I turn my life over to You. If I die I want to go to heaven. If I live, I'll be on the hook forever.'"

The patient's condition stabilized and he was later transported to another hospital. Today, this man is a strong Christian. Dr. Rawlings goes on to say, "I went home, dusted off my Bible and started reading it … This episode literally scared the hell out of me. It terrified me enough to write this book."

Here's one more example from Dr. Rawling's book. It's the story of a woman who was struck by lightning on a camping trip.

> "In the moment that I was hit," the woman says, "I knew exactly what had happened to me. My mind was crystal clear. I have never been so totally alive as in the act of dying."

> Isn't that interesting?

Regrets of past actions together with things she wanted to do in her life filled her mind.

> "At this point in the act of dying, I had what I call the answer to a question I had never verbalized to anyone—or even faced. The question was, 'Is there really a God?' I can't describe it, but the totality and reality of the living God exploded within my being. He filled every atom of my body with His glory. In the

next moment, to my horror, I found that I wasn't going toward God. I was going away from Him. It was like seeing what might have been, but going away from it. In my panic, I tried to start communicating with God—with the God I knew was there."

The book goes on to say she begged for her life and offered it to God, should He spare it. She recovered fully in three months and it changed her life.

■ Those Who Don't Know God

Those who don't believe, know, or obey God will also be on the "Who's Who" in hell list. When Jesus is revealed from heaven, He will punish those who do not know God and do not obey the Gospel of our Lord Jesus.

"God is just: He will pay back trouble to those who trouble you and give relief to you who are troubled,

and to us as well. This will happen when the Lord Jesus is revealed from heaven in blazing fire with his powerful angels. **He will punish those who do not know God and do not obey the gospel of our Lord Jesus. They will be punished with everlasting destruction and shut out from the presence of the Lord** and from the majesty of his power on the day he comes to be glorified in his holy people and to be marveled at among all those who have believed. This includes you, because you believed our testimony to you," (2 Thessalonians 1:6-10, NIV).

It's a sobering reality. Unbelievers and rebels against God will find themselves shut out from God's presence in hell.

■ Hell's Roster

Can you see that in addition to the devil and demons, hell has quite a sad membership roll? God gives us the profile of hell's guest list. The

Bible is pretty specific. Sadly, those who habitually practice these things and have no desire to repent, turn from sin, and live to please God will be on hell's roster.

*"But **cowards who turn away from me, and unbelievers, and the corrupt, and murderers, and the immoral, and those who practice witchcraft, and idol worshipers, and all liars—their doom is in the lake that burns with fire** and sulfur . . . ,"* (Revelation 21:8, NLT).

*"When you follow the desires of your sinful nature, your lives will produce these evil results: **sexual immorality, impure thoughts, eagerness for lustful pleasure, idolatry, participation in demonic activities, hostility, quarreling, jealousy, outbursts of anger, selfish ambition, divisions, the feeling that everyone is wrong except those in your own little group, envy, drunkenness, wild parties, and other kinds***

of sin. Let me tell you again, as I have before, that anyone living that sort of life will not inherit the Kingdom of God," (Galatians 5:19-21, NLT).

There is no room for throwing stones at others because if it were not for God's grace and the blood of Jesus, all of us would be on this list. When we surrender to Jesus Christ, confess Him as Lord, and walk in the light of His Word, He forgives us and removes our name from hell's roster. Listen to what God's Word says about the wages of sin and the abundant mercy He offers for those who repent.

"Don't you know that those who do wrong will have no share in the Kingdom of God? Don't fool yourselves. Those who indulge in **sexual sin, who are idol worshipers, adulterers, male prostitutes, homosexuals, thieves, greedy people, drunkards, abusers, and**

swindlers—*none of these will have a share in the Kingdom of God forget.* **There was a time when some of you were just like that, but now your sins have been washed away**, *and you have been set apart for God.* **You have been made right with God because of what the Lord Jesus Christ and the Spirit of our God have done for you,"** (I Corinthians 6:9-11, NLT).

God gives us some encouragement and a warning in Ephesians 5:6-8. *"Don't be fooled by those who try to excuse these sins, for the terrible anger of God comes upon all those who disobey him. Don't participate in the things these people do.* **For though your hearts were once full of darkness, now you are full of light from the Lord, and your behavior should show it!,"** (NLT).

Notice the bold sentences in the previous passages. There was a time when many of us were just like all the things described. Our hearts were full of darkness; BUT because of Jesus Christ, our sins have been washed away and now our behavior reflects our relationship with Him.

We were all guilty, but God had mercy on us when we believed in and received Jesus Christ. Because of His shed blood on the cross, our sins have been forgiven and we've been made right with God. God's not holding anything against us. Our name has been removed from hell's roster!

That is good news!

Chapter Four

■ Who's Who In Hell – Part 2

Can you see that hell is not going to be a big party? Hell's guest list is not anything we want to be on. The Bible has more to say about "Who's Who" in hell. Let's check it out.

It's not gonna be a party.

■ Rebellious, Big Shots On Earth

Rebellious, big shots will end up in hell. This is very interesting. The Bible tells us about a big reception in hell to celebrate the arrival of

Lucifer. On the day when he is thrown into hell and the lake of fire prepared for him, there will be a big reception to greet him. Listen to who's been assigned as "greeters" in hell.

"The denizens of hell crowd to meet you as you enter their domain. ***World leaders and earth's mightiest kings, long dead, are there to see you.*** With one voice they all cry out, 'Now you are as weak as we are!' Your might and power are gone; they are buried with you. All the pleasant music in your palace has ceased; now maggots are your sheet, worms your blanket! ***How you are fallen from heaven, O Lucifer, son of the morning!*** How you are cut down to the ground—mighty though you were against the nations of the world. ***For you said to yourself, 'I will ascend to heaven and rule the angels. I will take the highest throne. I will preside on the Mount of Assembly far away in the north. I will climb to the highest heavens***

and be like the Most High.' But instead,
you will be brought down to the pit of hell,
down to its lowest depths. *Everyone there will*
stare at you and ask, 'Can this be the one
who shook the earth and the kingdoms of
the world?,'" (Isaiah 14:9-16, TLB).

The hosts of hell will be the big shots on earth! World leaders, earth's mightiest kings—without Christ—get to be on the Welcome Team in hell. How the tables turn, after this life!

Other translations of the Bible describe these world leaders and mighty kings as "chief ones of the earth," "leaders in the world," "famous names of the earth," and "kings of the nations."

A person's status changes dramatically—if they do not know God—once they die and leave their body. While on earth they may have been a mighty, famous, influential, and wealthy "mover and shaker"; but if they didn't know Jesus Christ as Lord, they will end up working the name badge table in hell.

In the afterlife, things change.

If a person doesn't know Jesus Christ as their Lord, they don't have the Son; and if they don't have the Son, they don't have the eternal life God offered them.

*"And this is what God has testified: He has given us eternal life, and this life is in his Son. **So whoever has God's Son has life; whoever does not have his Son, does not have life,"** (1 John 5:11-12, NLT).*

We live in the age of human idolatry! Celebrities, stars, political figures, sports icons, business moguls, kings and queens, and princes and princesses are worshipped. Without Jesus Christ, it's all vanity and vapors that will soon fade away.

Thankfully, there are Godly leaders—those with influence, power, and wealth who use their platform to glorify God and advance the Gospel of Jesus Christ; those that use their position of power to feed the poor, heal the sick, and honor Jesus Christ. These are the kind of leaders we need!

We ought to pray that more and more of "the chief ones of the earth" come to know Jesus Christ and live a life that is pleasing to Him.

■ Those Who Take The Wrong Road

Those who don't take God's path will end up in hell. Jesus said many people would make the wrong choice. Listen to what Jesus said. *"Enter through the narrow gate.* **For wide is the gate and broad is the road that leads to destruction and many enter through it.**

But small is the gate and narrow the road that leads to life, and only a few find it," (Matthew 7:13-14, NIV).

The gate to heaven is not small because God only allows a few people to find it. It's small because there's only one way to heaven and eternal life. "Jesus answered, *I am the way and the truth and the life. No one comes to the Father except through me,'*" (John 14:6, NIV).

Did you know . . .

There are a lot of ways to get to hell? Sure, you can find many roads that will take you to hell, but Jesus said there's only one way to get to heaven. He's the way. Are you following Him?

▮ Average Joe

Who else will find themselves in hell? Those who don't have a reservation for heaven!

If a person's name has not been written in the Lamb's Book of Life, they will not be given an entrance into heaven.

Don't die and arrive at the pearly gates expecting to be seated at your heavenly table, only to find that heaven does not see your name in God's reservation book.

Can you imagine this scenario?

Average Joe dies and stands before heaven's angelic maitre' d and says, *"Yes, my name is Average Joe and I have a reservation for one."*

There is a pause as the angel scans the Book of Life searching for his name. The pause takes a bit longer as he begins a line-by-line search.

Finally, he looks up and says, *"I'm sorry, I don't see your name down for a reservation."*

"Well, there must be some mistake," Average Joe argues, a bit aggravated. *"My name should be there. I was a member of a church. I know I should have been more active. Okay, I probably didn't give enough, but my name was on their membership roster. I was a good person!"*

Heaven's maitre' d stands silently.

Average Joe begins to panic a bit, *"Yes, I know. I was too busy playing golf and hitting up the casino. I didn't make as much time for God in my life as I should have. I just thought all that "Jesus stuff" was a little bit fanatical . . . but, I'm here now and . . ."*

Average Joe begins to rationalize in a defensive manner, *"What? Yes, I did have a Bible. Actually, I had several Bibles . . . but do you know how busy I was? My job. Coaching sports. Reading the Wall Street Journal, and watching TV. I just wasn't that into reading the Bible . . ."*

Heaven's maitre' d stands silently.

Average Joe tries to be cute but is slightly angry. *"Hey, I'm here now. I've got all kind of time. I'll read my Bible and get to know God for eternity. Now, hurry up; just find my name, will ya?"*

As reality sets in, Average Joe calms down and begins to weep. *"Please, I'm begging you . . . If you could just check again? My name has to be in the Book of Life. Please, please, continue searching . . ."*

Heaven's maitre' d stands silently.

Average Joe becomes very defensive, *"What? No ... well, not exactly. I never officially surrendered to Jesus Christ. I believed in God and everything, but I wouldn't say Jesus was my Lord. I thought if I was just a good person that would be enough. You know . . . that's what everyone on Earth thinks . . ."*

Average Joe becomes extremely angry now. *"Yes, just cut the @#*, will you? Yes, I heard Bible stories as a kid. Jesus died on a cross. We drew pictures. What? No, I never gave it much thought. I don't know why He died on a cross; that was for religious people to figure out. Yes, I know it should have been more of a priority. So, what are you saying? Are you telling me that I do not have a reservation?"*

Heaven's maitre' d remains silent while showing Average Joe a Bible verse he didn't want to hear. *"And anyone whose name was not found recorded in the Book of Life was thrown into the lake of fire," (Revelation 20:15, NLT).*

Average Joe did not have a reservation. His name was not on God's guest list. His name was not found in the Book of Life. The last thing we heard from Average Joe was him cursing God in anger.

Can you see the importance of paying attention to God's priorities in this life? The importance of knowing God? The importance of the Book of Life?

This is one book you want to have your reservation recorded in! It doesn't matter that the local sports editor didn't write you up or that your name didn't appear in the company newsletter or in the *Who's Who of America*; but it makes an eternal difference if your name is not recorded in the Book of Life.

How different the reception will be for those whose names *are* written the Book of Life. They will receive a warm entrance into heaven.

"Nothing evil will be allowed to enter . . . but only those whose names are written in the Lamb's Book of Life," (Revelation 21:27, NLT).

*"Therefore, my brothers, be all the more eager to make your calling and election sure. For if you do these things, **you will never fall, and you will receive a rich welcome into the eternal kingdom of our Lord and Savior Jesus Christ,"*** (2 Peter 1:10-11, NIV).

You can make sure that you will "receive a rich welcome" into the eternal kingdom of our Lord and Savior Jesus Christ. You can make your "calling and election sure" by being certain that you have surrendered your life to the Lordship of Jesus Christ.

Have you?

Have you called on Jesus to be your personal Lord? Do you believe in your heart that God raised Jesus from the dead? Have you believed in and received Him into your life? If so, you can be sure that you are a child of God and your name is written in the Lamb's Book of Life. If not, I encourage you to surrender your heart to Jesus Christ and invite Him to be the Lord of your life.

Chapter Five

◼ What's What In Hell? – Part I

"C'mon, how bad can hell be? Where is hell? What goes on there? What does it look like?" People do wonder—what is hell like?

Do the words, "down, dirty, dark, dank, worms and wailing," tell you anything?

◼ Hell Is Down And Dirty

Hell is a place that's down and dark. People say, *"Where is hell, anyway?"* Where's it located? Physically, literally, where is hell?

The Bible tells us exactly where it is: *Down*.

"Therefore hell hath enlarged herself, and opened her mouth without measure: and their glory, and their multitude, and their pomp, and he that rejoiceth, shall **descend** *into it,"* (Isaiah 5:14, KJV).

Isaiah 14:9 says, **"Hell from beneath** *is excited about you, to meet you at your coming . . . ,"* (NKJV).

Jesus said, *"For as Jonah was three days and three nights in the belly of the great fish, so will the Son of Man be three days and three nights* **in the heart of the earth***,"* (Matthew 12:40, NKJV).

Literally, the Bible describes hell's location as being down. Jesus even more specifically said it was in "the heart of the earth," or as many theologians believe, in the center of the earth.

Interesting Facts.

The Earth. The earth's core is spinning separately from the rest of the planet. The earth's core is sitting within an outer shell of boiling liquid iron and the earth's center is 5,000-6,000 degrees.[1] That's interesting. Could hell be literally located at the center of the earth?

The Ocean. Listen to what Job said. *"**The dead tremble, those under the waters** and those inhabiting them. Sheol is naked before Him, and Destruction has no covering,"* (Job 26:5-6, NKJV).

*"**Have you entered the springs of the sea? Or have you walked in search of the depths? Have the gates of death been revealed to you? Or have you seen the doors of the shadow of death?** Have you comprehended the breadth of the earth? Tell Me, if you know all this,"* (Job 38:16-18, NKJV).

Job gives us the idea that the deceased tremble beneath the waters where the "gates of death" are located—or we'd say "beneath the oceans"—very likely, in hell.

Here are some more interesting facts: Ocean springs and hydrothermal vents were discovered in the last few decades. In 1977, they were found along the ridges of the ocean floor. They are known as *black smokers*. *"These black smokers are chimney-like structures made up of sulfur-bearing minerals or sulfides that come from beneath Earth's crust. They form when hot (roughly 350° C), mineral-rich water flows out onto the ocean floor through the volcanic lava on a mid-ocean ridge volcano."* Temperatures reach up to 403° Celsius.[2]

Interesting, isn't it? Who knows, maybe hell really is in the heart of the earth?

■ Hell Is Dark And Dank

Jude spells it out. *"For certain men have crept in unnoticed, who long ago were marked out for this condemnation, ungodly men, who turn the grace of our God into lewdness and deny the only Lord God and our Lord Jesus Christ. . . . These are spots in your love feasts, while they feast with you without fear, serving only themselves. They are clouds without water, carried about by the winds; late autumn trees without fruit, twice dead, pulled up by the roots; raging waves of the sea, foaming up their own shame; wandering stars for whom is reserved **the blackness of darkness forever**,"* (Jude 4, 12-13, NKJV). He describes hell as "the blackness of darkness forever."

How dark is dark?

Jesus called hell "outer darkness." *". . . cast him into **outer darkness**; there will be weeping and gnashing of teeth,"* (Matthew 22:13, NKJV).

The late Kenneth Hagin, Sr. wrote a book called, *I Went To Hell*, which describes his personal near-death experience of going to hell. He describes what he felt as he leapt out of his body.

> *"I began to descend, down, down into a pit, like you'd go down into a well, cavern, or cave. . . As I was trying to say goodbye, I knew I was going down into that place. All three of my family members who were present testified later saying, "When you said, 'Goodbye,' your voice sounded like you were way down in a cave or cavern or something." As I continued to descend, I went down feet first. Down, down, down, down. I could look up and see the lights of the Earth. They finally faded away. Darkness encompassed me round about—darkness that is darker than any night man has ever seen. It seemed that*

if you had a knife, you could cut a chunk of it out. You couldn't see your hand if it was one inch in front of your nose. The farther down I went, the darker it became and the hotter it became; until finally, way down beneath me, I could see the fingers of light playing on the wall of darkness and I came to the bottom of the pit. This happened to me more than 60 years ago, yet it is just as real to me as if it happened last week."[3]

◾ Hell Is A Place Of Worms And Wailing

The Bible describes hell as a place of worms and weeping.

Worms.

"Hell from beneath is excited about you, to meet you at your coming; it stirs up the dead for you, all the chief ones of the earth; it has raised up from their thrones all the kings of the nations. They all shall speak and say to you: 'Have you also become as weak as we? Have you become like us? Your pomp is brought down to Sheol, and the sound of your stringed instruments; **the maggot is spread under you, and worms cover you**,'" (Isaiah 14:9-11, NKJV).

It sounds disgusting and gross.

I remember even as a six-year-old kid wondering about the worms. If I was six feet under, would the worms get me?

Here's an interesting scientific fact they've discovered. Tubeworms, called riftia, are six to eight feet long and have been found at the ocean's floor near hydrothermal vents. They are like nothing on earth. These worms thrive in toxic chemicals, high temperatures, high pressure, and total darkness.[4] Mmmm . . . Jesus said hell is loaded with worms that don't die.

"If your hand causes you to sin, cut it off. It is better for you to enter into life maimed, rather than having two hands, to go to hell, into the fire that shall never be quenched—where **'Their worm does not die and the fire is not quenched,'"** (Mark 9:43-44, NKJV).

What else do we know about hell?

The Bible says that hell is also a place of wailing. *"So it will be at the end of the age. The angels will come forth, separate the wicked from among the just, and cast them into the furnace of fire.* **There will be wailing and gnashing of teeth,"** (Matthew 13:48-50, NKJV).

The wailing described here is a picture of great sobs, lamenting, wailing aloud as sign of pain and grief. Can you imagine the pain of regret that many people will feel when they realize what rejecting Jesus has cost them?

Hell is a real place. It's a terrifying place that you don't want to visit. Does the Bible tell us anything else about hell?

Chapter Six

■ What's What In Hell? – Part 2

Jesus had a lot to say about hell. Primarily, because He doesn't want anyone to go there!

Is there more? There is. It gets worse. The words, "teeth, torment, big and burning," come to mind.

■ Hell Is A Place Of Teeth And Torment

The Bible describes hell as a place of teeth and torment.

Jesus said, "'This is how it will be at the end of the age. The angels will come and separate the wicked from the righteous and throw them into the fiery furnace, where **there will be weeping and gnashing of teeth**," (Matthew 13:49-50, NIV).

The gnashing of teeth is, in part, a picture of remorse; people gnashing their teeth in remorse and anger.

Hell is also a place of torment.

*"There was a rich man who was dressed in purple and fine linen and lived in luxury every day. At his gate was laid a beggar named Lazarus, covered with sores and longing to eat what fell from the rich man's table. Even the dogs came and licked his sores. The time came when the beggar died and the angels carried him to Abraham's side. **The rich man also died and was buried.***

In hell, where he was in torment, he looked up and saw Abraham far away, with Lazarus by his side. So he called to him, '**Father Abraham, have pity on me and send Lazarus to dip the tip of his finger in water and cool my tongue, because I am in agony in this fire.**' But Abraham replied, 'Son, remember that in your lifetime you received your good things, while Lazarus received bad things, but now he is comforted here and you are in agony. And besides all this, between us and you a great chasm has been fixed, so that those who want to go from here to you cannot, nor can anyone cross over from there to us.' He answered, 'Then I beg you, father, send Lazarus to my father's house, for I have five brothers. Let him warn them, **so that they will not also come to this place of torment,**'"[3] (Luke 16:19-27, NIV).

This is probably one of the most descriptive stories about hell in the Bible. This story describes real people, the rich man and Lazarus. They both lived ... and they both died. The rich man went to hell where he was very alert. We see a couple of truths about the rich man's state of being while he was in hell:

- He was conscious.
- He could see.
- He was alert.
- He could speak.
- He prayed.
- He could taste.
- He was aware of his family.
- He was in agony.
- He was tormented.

A person doesn't cease to exist in hell. There is a very real awareness, great agony and torment.

■ Hell Is Big And Burning

Hell is growing!

It's a sad truth—hell is getting bigger!

*"Therefore **hell hath enlarged herself**, and opened her mouth without measure: and their glory, and their multitude, and their pomp, and he that rejoiceth, shall descend into it,"* (Isaiah 5:14, KJV).

If, according to statistics, 1.5 million Americans a year die without Christ and potentially go to a place called hell, then hell would have to be a big place. These figures don't even account for the rest of earth's population.

This is so tragic.

The Bible also tells us that hell is hot! *"And whosoever was not found written in the book of life was cast into **the lake of fire**,"* (Revelation 20:15, KJV). *"And if thy hand offend thee, cut it off: it is better for thee to enter into life maimed, than having two hands to go into hell, into **the fire that never shall be quenched:** Where their worm dieth not, and **the fire is not quenched,"** (Mark 9:43-44, KJV).*

> *I find this very sobering.*
> *Do you?*

I hope you're thinking about people you know; people you love and care about who may not know Christ. I pray that you are being stirred up and your heart is crying out, *"Oh God, I don't want anyone I know to go to hell. Help me convey Your love to my family and friends in a way that they'll understand."*

We all agree, people don't want to be preached at. They don't want to hear about "hellfire and brimstone," right? However, if the Bible is true, how can we keep the information to ourselves?

God help us!

■ Hell Has An Entrance But No Exit

Let's wrap up with this: hell has an entrance, but no exit. People "check-in," but they don't "check-out."

Jesus said, *". . . I will build my church; and **the gates of hell** shall not prevail against it,"* (Matthew 16:18, KJV).

The "gates of hell" describes an entrance as well as the authority of hell. Job 17:16 describes the "bars of death," as well. Again, a picture of an entrance, but not an exit. People without Christ will go away to eternal punishment behind bars and gates. Sounds like a prison doesn't it?

We cannot even begin to imagine the concept of being locked up for eternity. This was never God's plan.

Don't go there.

It's true. The Bible describes a place called hell, but it was originally prepared for the devil and his demons. God doesn't want anyone to go to hell, but He will not violate our free will and force us to choose Jesus Christ.

We can go to hell, if we want to. My prayer, as you have read the basic facts about hell, is that your heart is turning toward the Lord in a genuine way. I pray you are moved to surrender your life to Jesus Christ. I hope you will allow Him to wash all your sins away and spend the rest of your life—and eternity—walking with Him.

Chapter Seven

■ Why This Is Important To Me

This topic of *hell* hits home with me for several reasons . . . my own life and the lives of those I love.

■ My Background

I was raised as a Roman Catholic. I am thankful for my upbringing as a Catholic. As a kid, I liked going to Mass; figuring out when to stand, sit, kneel; making my first communion, first confession, confirmation, and going to CCD. I really kinda liked the whole thing.

I don't remember receiving any particular godly "lightening bolt" from attending church. I just liked the "religiousness" of it all. Probably, the biggest thing that hit me in church as a kid was a general awareness and respect for God.

When I was about ten years old, I quit going to church when my parents split up. I drifted for about ten years. I still believed in God, tried to get to church occasionally, and worked on being a good person; but my focus was on living the party life!

During my teen and high school years, I played by my own rules. As a good Catholic, I figured there wasn't anything I could do that a couple of "Our Father's" and a few "Hail Mary's" wouldn't fix. My faith was pretty shallow.

■ My Conversion

Things started to change my freshman year in college. My roommate (a childhood friend) talked to me about having a personal relationship with Jesus Christ. Something had happened to her; she found Jesus.

She "witnessed" to me, a lot. I wanted to talk about smoking Marlboro's, drinking Miller Light and being Catholic; she wanted to talk about knowing Jesus. She got me thinking, so I started to read the Bible for the first time in my life.

God began to get a hold of my heart.

It's a long story; but within nine months of beginning to read the Bible, I made a decision to surrender my heart to God and personally invite Jesus to be the Lord of my life.

It was THE defining moment of my life.

I didn't hear the angels sing or see the heavens part. I didn't feel one "goose-bump," but I did receive an immediate sense that I had peace with God.

I discovered later that the decision to surrender my life to Jesus Christ had made me a "born again Christian." Where I had been "religious" before, I now had a "relationship" with Jesus Christ.

I couldn't get enough of the Bible. I had no idea the Bible said so much about what a personal relationship with Jesus Christ meant. Developing a friendship with the Lord and discovering all that the Bible said was like unlocking a treasure chest. I couldn't believe how good the Good News was!

Not only did knowing Jesus give me a new sense of peace, happiness, and contentment; but I was also pleasantly surprised to discover the Bible promised me that because of my relationship with Jesus, when I died, I would go to heaven.

As a freshman in college, with my new-found faith and a fresh understanding that heaven and hell were real destinations; I wanted everyone to know Jesus and the way to God's heaven!

My experience in coming to Christ was dramatic and life-changing. I wanted to tell the whole world about Jesus! It was the premier thing in my heart and I was moved to begin praying for my family and friends. I frequently asked the Lord, *"How can I share all of this with my family?"*

Perhaps, as a believer, you've experienced this same passionate zeal and have been accused of being some type of "Jesus freak." Sometimes, our family (and friends) only knows us as "us." They only know the "heathen" us—how we were *before* we got saved—so they don't always understand this "born again" thing. In their minds, we just got more religious and became some kind of a fanatic!

That's what my family thought.

■ My Family's Reaction

I really felt pretty inept at sharing my faith. I desperately wanted to tell my family and friends about Jesus, but it just didn't seem to come out right until ...

... the summer of 1979.

I was out East on a summer project with a campus ministry. Me and about fifty other college students lived in a giant beach house in Hampton Beach, New Hampshire. For thirteen weeks we were "missionaries" sharing our faith on the beach, working in discipleship teams, praying for the community, and hosting outreach events—all the while, growing in our relationship with the Lord. What a summer!

My family thought I had dropped off the deep end. My mom and two of my sisters decided to travel to Hampton Beach for a visit just to make sure I hadn't joined some cult like the Moonies. To say my mother was "concerned" would be an understatement. As it turned out, it was a life-changing visit for my whole family.

One day, on a road trip from Hampton Beach to Boston, we were all talking about the summer project and *"God-stuff"* when my mom asked a question about heaven. I told her the one verse I really knew, John 14:6. *"Mom,"* I began, "Jesus said, *'I am the way and the truth and the life. No one comes to the Father except through me.'"*

My mom's response was, *"You mean to tell me, if I don't accept Jesus Christ as my personal Lord and Savior I will spend eternity in hell?"* I couldn't believe she had connected the dots so quickly.

Her response surprised me!

I replied, *"Yes, Mom. I didn't say it; Jesus said it. I mean, these are not my words. Jesus made this statement. He said, 'I am the way and the truth and the life. No one comes to the Father except through me.'"*

She responded for the second time, *"You mean to tell me . . . if I don't accept Jesus Christ as my personal Lord and Savior, I will spend eternity in hell?"*

Again, I said, *"Yes Mom, I didn't say it. Jesus said it. I'm just telling you what Jesus said. He said, 'I am the way and the truth and the life.' No one comes to the Father except through Him."*

For the third time, she responded with more passion than before, *"You mean to tell me ... if I don't accept Jesus Christ as my personal Lord and Savior, I will spend eternity in hell?"*

Again, I said, *"Yes, Mom, I didn't say it. Jesus said it."*

> *Her next statement*
> *totally shocked me.*

I was prepared for one of two responses: First, I was prepared for my mom to say, *"Well I don't believe that. How could a loving God send anyone to hell?"*

Secondly, I was prepared for her to say, *"Well, I don't believe that. What about all the people in Africa and remote jungles, that haven't heard about Jesus?"*

I was prepared to answer both of those classic arguments, but she didn't say either one!

Here's what she did say: *"If you believe that I would spend eternity in hell if I didn't accept Jesus Christ as my personal Lord and Savior, then why did it take you a year and a half to tell me and your family?"*

> *That sobered me.*
> *She got it!*

What I heard in her words was, *"What is wrong with you? Why didn't you tell me this information the minute you got it? Were you going to let me go to hell?"*

She understood the magnitude of the whole deal. She got it. If Jesus was Who He said He was and if His Words were true, why did it take me so long to get this Good News to my family?

The end of the story is simply this. A short time later, she received Jesus as her Lord and so did the rest of my family!

■ My Motivation

That conversation has been a huge motivator for me ever since. It's what moves me to preach, teach, write, and work with my husband to pastor an outreach-oriented church.

I don't want to be found guilty
of withholding the Good News.

To tell you the truth, if I was unsaved and someone I knew had this information, I'd give them a big kick in the rear if they didn't tell me!

There are a lot of things we can focus on as Christians, but let's never lose the primary purpose to which God has called us—making sure the people we know and love do not go to hell!

How could a loving God send anyone to hell? I hope you've seen that a loving God doesn't! In His kindness, He gives us a choice to accept or reject the free gift of eternal life He offers through His son.

I hope you choose Jesus.

Chapter Eight

■ One Final Question

I'm glad you've read this book. I have one more thing I want you to share with you. As we've discussed, one of the most important issues in all of life is knowing where you will spend eternity. Do you know for sure where you'll go when you die?

> *Do you know*
> *Jesus Christ?*

If not, God has provided the way to eternal life—through His Son, Jesus Christ. Our apathy or blatant rebellion—known as sin—separates us from Him. Jesus came to bridge that great divide by dying on a cross. He took the penalty for our sin and He offers us the free gift of forgiveness so that we can be reconciled with God. Would you like to make things right with God today and be certain of your eternal destiny?

Jesus is standing at the door of your heart and if you will surrender your life to Him, He will forgive all your sins and write your name in the Lamb's Book of Life. Are you ready to invite Jesus into your life? If so, simply pray this prayer, from your heart:

Dear God,

I need You in my life. I have sinned and I ask You to forgive me. Jesus, I believe You are alive and real. I surrender my heart to You. At this very moment, I invite You into my life, to be the Lord of my life now and eternally. I ask You to help me get to know you better and help me become the person you have created me to be. In Jesus' Name. Amen.

If you prayed this prayer, I encourage you to do three things:

1. Start reading the New Testament.

2. Start talking to Jesus from your heart to His.

3. Start attending a Spirit-filled Bible church.

3 Things.

Conversation Starters

Chapter One
1. Why do you think people are in denial about hell?

2. What ideas have you heard about hell?

Chapter Two
1. Talk about the difference between the "fire and brimstone" approach to hell and a healthy fear of hell.

2. Describe the "Mapquest" God has given us for getting to heaven.

Chapter Three
1. What do you think about the "life after death" experiences people have had?

2. Who does the Bible say is on hell's guest list?

Chapter Four
1. After this life, how do the tables turn for big shots and those that don't know Christ?

2. Talk about these Bible verses that describe having a reservation for heaven: Revelation 20:15, Revelation 21:27, and 2 Peter 1:10. Do you have one?

Study Guide

Conversation Starters

Chapter Five

1. Talk about the Scriptures that describe hell as being "down" and possibly in the center of the earth.

2. Discuss the concepts of "down and dirty," "dark and dank," and "worms and wailing."

Chapter Six

1. Read Luke 16:19-28 and discuss the description of hell.

2. Talk about the eternal nature of hell; people check in and they don't check out. How does this motivate you?

Chapter Seven

1. Share your personal story of conversion to Christ.

2. Talk about how your family has reacted to your faith.

Chapter Eight

1. Have you received Jesus as Lord? Would you like to?

2. Share a little about your walk and journey with Jesus.

Bibliography

Works Cited

Chapter Two

1 Jones, Beth. *DEATH: What Happens Next?* Portage, MI: Beth Jones Ministries, 2007, www.bethjones.org.

2 http://www.itsmylife.com/statistics.asp

3 http://www.barna.org

Chapter Three

1 Rawlings, Maurice. *Beyond Death's Door.* Nashville, TN: Bantam, 1991.

Chapter Five

1 http://www.en.wikipedia.org/wiki/Inner_core

2 http://www.amnh.org/nationalcenter/expeditions/blacksmokers/black_smokers.html

3 Hagin, Kenneth. *I Went To Hell.* Tulsa, OK: Faith Library Publications, 1982.

4 http://www.seasky.org/monsters/sea7a1g.html; http://www.extremescience.com/deepcreat5.htm

Other Resources

Get A Grip Mini-Books: The Question Series

HELL - How could a loving God send anyone there?

DEATH - What happens next?

SICKNESS - What does God think about it?

HEALING - How does God do it?

SUFFERING - Why does God allow it?

WOMEN - What's their role in church?

EASTER - Why the gory, bloody cross?

Getting A Grip On The Basics Bible Study Series:

Getting A Grip On The Basics

Getting A Grip On The Basics Of Serving God

Getting A Grip On The Basics Of Health And Healing

Getting A Grip On The Basics Of Prosperous Living

Getting A Grip On The Basics For Kids

Getting A Grip On The Basics For Teens

Getting A Grip On The Basics – Spanish

Bite Sized Bible Studies Series:

Satisfied Lives For Desperate Housewives

Kissed or Dissed

The Friends God Sends

Don't Factor Fear Here

What To Do When You Feel Blue

Grace For The Pace

Bite Sized Bible Studies DVD Curriculum:

Satisfied Lives For Desperate Housewives

Don't Factor Fear Here

Grace For The Pace